The Backpacker series is lovingly dedicated to
Noreen Bridgen, Jennifer MacAulay, John Denison and my
Radical Teachers mastermind group for their brilliance,
experience and unfailing support.

JUDY THOMPSON

Backpacker's Guide to Teaching English

CRACKING THE CODE
BOOK ONE

PRONUNCIATION

Thompson Language Center
Niagara Falls, Canada

Copyright © 2018 by Judy Thompson.
Second Edition 2021. Third Edition 2026.

Developed in Canada

ISBN: 978-0-9812058-4-7

CIP available upon request.

Every effort has been made to trace ownership of all copyrighted material and to secure permission from copyright holders. In the event of any question arising as to the use of any material, we would be pleased to make the necessary corrections in future printings.

Edited by: Noreen Brigden and Jennifer MacAulay

Cover design by: McCorkindale Advertising & Design

Layout and Production by: McCorkindale Advertising & Design

Graph and chart updates: Gillian Stead

Printed in USA (subject to change)

TLC THOMPSON LANGUAGE CENTER

Contents

RUSSIA

IMMIGRATION

1234

1234

DEPARTURE

SEP 2010

15 DEC 2010

09 MAY

ARRIVAL

ARRIV INDIA

ARRIVAL

0 : 12 : 2010

BRAZIL

0123

CHINA

20 AUG 2016

DEPARTED

123

0123

CANADA

AUG 2016

RIVAL

ARRIVED

USA

TXL

ABC

Backpacker's Guide to Teaching English

CRACKING THE CODE BOOK ONE

Book One

Pronunciation

By Judy Thompson

You can't speak English from reading it.

Circumstances create informal English instructors that the English as a Second Language (ESL) industry calls Backpackers. Although the term was originally coined for travelers, it can apply to volunteers, refugee hosts, any people with no special teacher training who find themselves in a position to assist non-native speakers improve their English but with no idea how to do it. While coaching with no formal training sounds like a brazen, formidable task, it isn't. It's a snap. And having no special education for it is a blessing in disguise.

— Judy Thompson

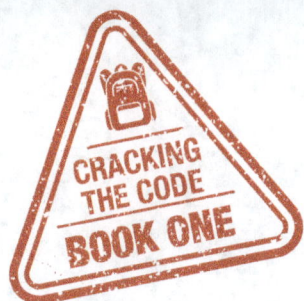

Introduction

The secret to teaching English effectively is being able to **harvest what is the same** about English and any learner's first language. The secret to comparing languages is understanding the simple framework of one language in order to measure others against it. The lowest common denominator between languages is sounds. In this book are the **sounds** of General American English (GA), a simple way to represent the **pronunciation** of GA with the **English Phonetic Alphabet** (EPA), and the **tools to compare** these sounds to the sounds of any other language.

When I say English, I mean **spoken English.** I've never met a non-native speaker, regardless of their fluency level, who didn't want to speak English more accurately and confidently. The global demand for English instruction is so intense, travellers, volunteers, host families... virtually any native English or fluent English speaker may be pressed upon to help someone with their English at some time. Casual teachers are often very effective, which upsets formally trained teachers to no end. While the English as a Second Language (ESL) industry has disdainfully dubbed informal teachers **Backpackers,** its own track record for language education has consistently been so poor, *no traditional training in it* turns out to be a bonus. This book is for budding teachers, regardless of their education, who need or want to make a profound difference in the speaking ability of learners.

The **Code** is a reference to English spelling. For reasons we'll touch on soon, the alphabet (spelling) doesn't make any sense in English. Some of you are breathing a sigh of relief that it has finally been said out loud; some of you are up in arms in knee-jerk defence of your mother tongue. The rest of you are somewhere in between. For the second group, take a deep breath! I am not attacking English: I am addressing it. *Red, head* and *said* should not rhyme, but they do (dew, due). *Few* and *sew* should rhyme, but they don't. Spelling is the code that gets cracked here, and it has to be cracked before anyone can learn to speak English from reading it.

If you are a certified ESL or English teacher taking a peek behind the curtain at this uncomplicated system for teaching speaking, good for you, but you had better put your big girl/boy pants on because we are going to ride roughshod over what is currently wrong with language education for a few paragraphs then we are done. (In fact, unless you have the hide of a rhino, step away from the book.)

The Purposes of This Book

The purposes of this text are threefold:

1 To establish beyond a shadow of a doubt that English writing and English speaking are separate and distinct languages

2 To supply a functional phonetic alphabet (EPA) to represent the 40 sounds of General American English (GA)

3 To provide tools for easily identifying differences between GA sounds and those of any other language

My Story

In my youth, I hiked and traveled extensively all over the world. As a Canadian and native English speaker, wherever I went, people would ask me if I would help them with their English. I wanted to help but wasn't sure how. Mostly, I chatted with them to give them practice and/or pointed out one or two errors that leapt out at me in conversation. I always felt badly I couldn't help them more.

Eventually, I put away my hiking boots, earned a degree, got married, had children, and became an English as a Second Language (ESL) teacher. Twice my career took me to Korea for three-month stints where I taught post-graduate students, middle schoolboys and English teachers. Time was of the essence in Korea. I spent a third of my time there traveling and two months teaching. To serve my students efficiently, I stopped trying to teach them everything I'd learned about English and only taught them the parts of English that were most critical for them to know. A whole new world of effectiveness opened up when I asked myself, *Can I powerfully affect my students' relationship to English for the rest of their lives in less than eight hours of class time?* The answer was a resounding *Yes!* but not by using any book or material that currently existed.

The Backpacker's Guide to Teaching English series was written for travelers and others who find themselves in the same boat I was many years ago, wanting to make a profound, positive difference in a stranger's ability to speak English in a very short time.

CRACKING THE CODE BOOK ONE

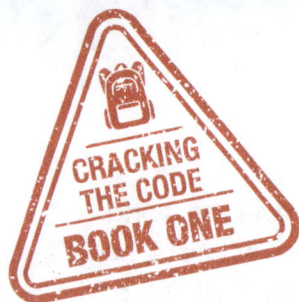

Conversation Backstory

Communication is made of layers of elements from individual sounds and sounds strung together as words, phrases and expressions, to gestures, voice qualities, and most importantly **context**. It's a lot of information. So where do we start?

Context is everything, so let's begin with the context for language learning in general, then English specifically.

There are three tenets that provide the context for this approach. You have to totally accept all three or there is no point reading on.

1) Pattern Learning

'Humans are pattern-seeking, meaning-making machines'

Rita Baker — Brain Power

Everything people learn is by finding patterns that are always true. We don't wash dishes before we fill the sink. Hot water works better than cold. Soap helps. Cleanest to dirtiest: glassware, cutlery, bowls, plates, pots and pans... Even if we aren't specifically taught a process like washing dishes or speaking a first language, humans are hard-wired to figure out quickly what works and discard what doesn't. Here is the kicker **as soon as we become proficient at any task, we forget how we did it.** Once humans learn a behaviour, the 'how to' step slips below our level of awareness into our subconscious, quietly running our dishwashing and conversation programs for the rest of our days. We never have to think about how to walk, wash dishes, tie shoes, drive a car, speak our first language... unless we go to teach them.

The breakdown in traditional language education has been to ignore that humans are pattern thinkers and teach onerous, meaningless, usually inaccurate *details* about language instead. Having students memorize information then reproduce the data on tests is exactly why language learning has historically been such a mind-numbing waste of time for learners and a juicy, big, fat, enduring cash-cow for publishers and institutions.

Traditional education is bad news for learners but good news for Backpackers. Your approach to helping others speak English hasn't been poisoned by outdated teacher education. You are starting fresh with only *pattern information* that can really help learners quickly. Lucky you!

2) What's Weird About English

All languages make sense except English. FYI, languages are spoken before they are written, and this part is true of English as well. Where English went off the tracks was when it was initially written down. Normally, when languages are written down, a system of symbols is contrived — one symbol for each sound, so people can **read the sounds** to speak a language by reading it and/or writing it down from how it sounds. **Alphabets are created to bridge speaking and writing.** This is the part that didn't happen with English.

Without going into too much detail (that you wouldn't remember anyway), in 1476, William Caxton bought a printing press from a trade show and started writing English down. In Caxton's time, English had been spoken for about 1,000 years, was largely a combination of German, Norse and French, and used about **40 sounds.** Caxton borrowed the **26 symbol** Latin alphabet (ABCs) without adding any extra symbols for the 14 unrepresented sounds. It's his fault **to, two** and **too** rhyme with **do, due** and **dew** but not **go** or **no** or **know.** He made a mess. English spelling has been random from day one (won), and we have been copying one man's spelling mistakes for over 500 years.

It gets worse. The education system completely steps over the fact that English doesn't make sense and teaches as if it did! **Sound it out** remember that? — the single most destructive phrase in Education history. English is a non-phonetic language; letters don't make sense. You can't speak English from reading it.

No wun kan sawn dingli shawt.

If a native English speaker somehow figures out how to read, that human brain thing kicks in, and *they forget how they did it!* We believe we learned to read from something our teachers said or did, when in fact those of us who did learn to read did it despite what our teachers said or did.

In English, it all goes back to the dysfunctional alphabet. Because our first language is acquired before we go to school, we don't study listening or speaking in school; we study reading and writing exclusively. The alphabet, spelling, printing, grammar, punctuation, capitalization, literature, composition... are all reading and writing skills. There is no bridge connecting the writing skills we learned in school to spoken English, none whatsoever. English speaking and English writing are totally separate, remember? Very weird! It does explain how students sit in English class for eons and never learn to speak English. Until this book, neither native speakers nor ESL teachers had any idea how conversation works.

Studying reading and writing skills in other languages makes perfect sense. Nordic countries in particular have the highest adult literacy scores in the world. Where language is logical, reading is no big deal. Symbols are a reflection of the language the learners already speak.

I'm not sure if I'm flogging a dead horse here, but check out this Adult Literacy chart put forth by the Conference Board of Canada.

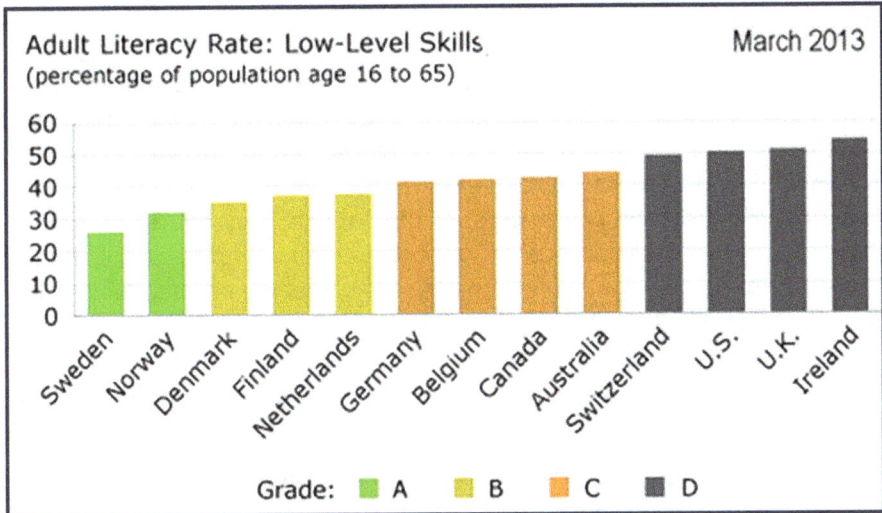

Adult Literacy Rate: Low-Level Skills
(percentage of population age 16 to 65)

March 2013

Grade: A B C D

(http://www.conferenceboard.ca/hcp/Details/education/adult-literacy-rate-lowskills.aspx?
AspxAutoDetectCookieSupport=1)

The Nordic countries are doing extremely well, with A and B grades. These are countries where alphabets make sense. The best any English speaking country achieved was Canada followed closely by Australia with Cs and the rest with Ds. (I'm sure we only published it because we did better than America, and that is all we really care about.) It is not a coincidence that no English-speaking country can excel in literacy because of the disconnect between speaking and writing — no logical alphabet. The already bad situation is compounded by how poorly it is addressed by the education system as in, not at all. The entire mess is topped off with the cheap trick of blaming the students when they don't get it.

Why all this matters to Backpackers is because people who are learning English from you are coming from a place of logic. Other languages make sense. This is the language software learners are bringing to the table, and you have to start where they are. It is up to you as their coach to set them straight about English and reassure them that you can sort out this crazy language for them. **Being straight about English not making sense is validating for learners and lends credibility to you.** Your students already know English is crazy; your stock goes up as soon as you admit it.

3) All Languages are the Same.

Okay, that is a little overstated, but any polyglot will tell you **languages are more the same than different.** This is the good stuff. Traditionally, ESL students have been staunchly discouraged from using their first language. **We have been teaching ESL as if learners were mute, and the truth is every student already uses most of the sounds they need for English.** The old approach is soul-crushing, ineffective and unprofessional. It fosters bored, unhappy students who achieve little. What we need to do instead is determine which parts of the student's first language are the same as in English and focus on teaching only the few parts that are different, as in missing. You can start to see the efficiency of this method for teaching and learning.

All major languages use about 40 sounds, and any two languages share almost exactly the same set of sounds! In this book, we are getting the sounds of English down. Then we will have a reference point and be able to identify what is the same about English and any other language. We only teach the tiny parts that are different.

Recap the Three Tenets:

1 Human brains learn by finding patterns that are always true and promptly forgetting exactly *how* they learned a skill once they have mastered it.

2 Written English and spoken English are unconnected by a logical alphabet, so you can't speak English from reading it.

3 Any two languages share almost the same sets of sounds and are fundamentally more the same than different. The best way to learn a new language is by identifying the parts that are similar, then teaching only the bits that aren't.

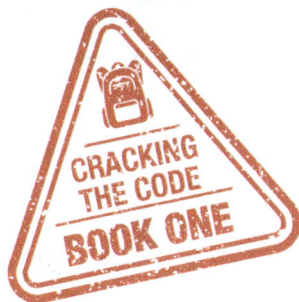

The Context for Learning to Speak English

1 Written and Spoken English are Completely Different Languages.

They always have been. A short foray into the *History of English* is well worth the time for you and your students. Don't nod off just because you read the word *history*. This is actually pretty interesting for everyone, and extremely validating for learners (something they are not used to in English class, so it is a positive start to your relationship). I can't count the number of ESL classes I've taught over the years, and I started every one with the *History of English*, which I like to call ***How English Came to be so Messed Up.***

The history of **Spoken English** is the red line at the top. The vertical rectangle in the middle is the part that concerns your students. This was the moment when Caxton wrote English down using the wrong alphabet and ruined English for everyone. Instead of taking the 26-symbol Latin or Roman alphabet or ABCs (whatever you want to call it) and adding 14 symbols to represent the shortfall, he winged it. He just winged spelling. Sometimes he used the spelling from the original language, but mostly he made it up. **Written English** as depicted by the black line at the bottom started in 1476.

THE HISTORY OF ENGLISH

Spoken English   40 sounds

Angles
Saxons
Jutes   William
                          the
German   +   Vikings   Conqueror   +   William Caxton
               Norse   French   Printing Press   Sir Isaac Newton   Bill Gates   Global English
                                              World languages + Science + Technology

450   800   1066   1476   1603   1945   2008
                                                          1684   1981

ᚠᚢᚦᚨᚱᚲ   Catholic Church |—
Runes   Latin ABC   Dictionary
                                                                        BBM
                                                                                             Texting

Written English   26 letters

                                                        Written English for common people

Old English   Middle English   Modern English   Global English

WILLIAM CAXTON SEPARATES WRITING FROM SPEAKING 1476

TLC THOMPSON LANGUAGE CENTER

© Judy Thompson 2026   www.thompsonlanguagecenter.com

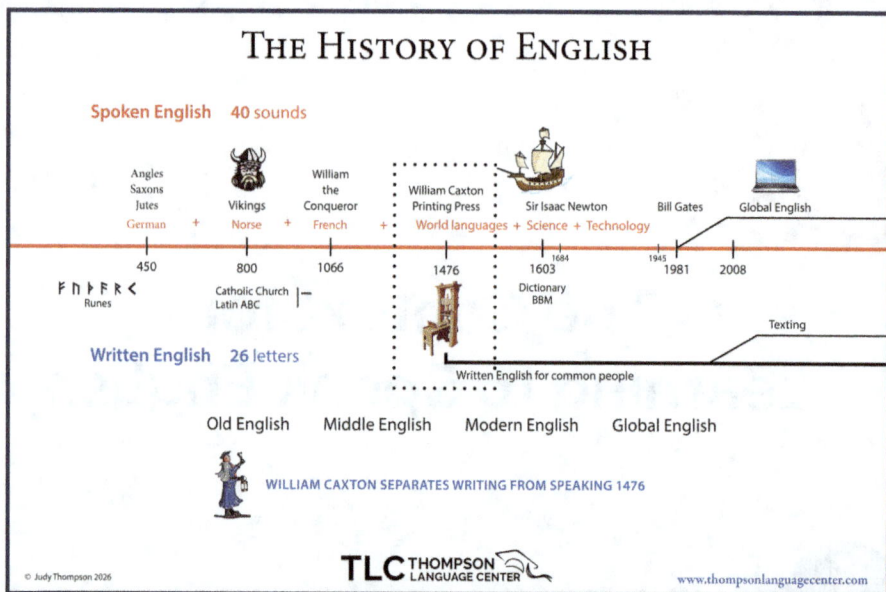

Learners need to know that English letters never represented English sounds. "English has a non-phonetic alphabet" is the fancy way of saying there isn't enough information in written English to speak it. If English is your first language, you might be feeling a little affronted right now, but non-native English speakers are starting to feel great.

To add insult to injury, the Western (Western is very kind, it was British) education system only taught reading and writing because listening and speaking were in place before native speakers went to school. Every other English-speaking colony or nation copied them. (Copying without updating — how Caxtonian; it's the lazy educator's shortcoming.) When native speakers started teaching ESL or *English* as they liked to call it, all they really taught was reading and writing because it was all they knew. Everything your students ever learned in school was about reading and writing and had nothing whatsoever to do with speaking. This is why learners have had so much trouble learning to speak English confidently no one ever taught them how. There isn't an ESL teacher in a hundred thousand who even knows how.

I strongly suggest your first lesson include that **History of English** chart or scratching a long horizontal timeline on a piece of paper, the board or a stretch of sand and marking it with a few key events in English Language history:

450 AD   German-speaking Angles, Saxons and Jutes conquer the British Isles, thenceforth known as *Angleland.*

800 AD   Norse arrive, fight, no winner and the cultures combine creating a new language known as **Old English.** It was the beginning of two or more unrelated words that mean exactly the same thing: anger/wrath, skin/hide, sick/ill... FYI, the Norse also gifted us with the silly 's' in the third person singular of the simple present: He eats.

1066 AD   William the Conqueror conquered and French was added to the mix. Among other things, the resulting **Middle English** supplied even more words for exactly the same thing. (Other languages don't do this.)

So far, English is only a spoken language and well on its way to becoming the biggest language ever.

1476   **Doomsday.** William Caxton wrote English down and made the mess known as **Modern English.** Printing houses popped up and every printer spelled words differently, adding and subtracting letters at random to justify their margins. William Caxton singlehandedly split English into speaking and writing.

1603   Society decided to standardize spelling and put all of Caxton's spelling mistakes in a big, fat book called the Dictionary, or as I like to call it, the **Big Book of Mistakes** (BBM).

The rest doesn't matter, but it is interesting that in 1684, Isaac Newton and his physics cronies realized they all spoke English. Forthwith, English became the language of science and education, replacing Latin.

1982   Bill Gates launched Microsoft and the impact on English was immeasurable. The language of technology, Global or **International English** dawned.

Is this a pattern or a heck of a coincidence? Three different Williams ushered in each new era of English: 1066, **William** the Conqueror, Middle English; 1476, **William** Caxton, Modern English; and 1982, **William** Gates, International English. Coincidence? You don't need to share this with students, but I promised it was going to be interesting.

Interesting is not the reason you will share all or more likely parts of this chart with your students. You share it to provide **context.** It authenticates what learners have already studied and explains that English is seriously flawed and there is nothing wrong with them. They can see they have only studied reading and writing, and this is why they can't speak . You'll teach them to speak. No pressure.

Just as importantly, the **History of English** lesson gives your students a chance to **listen to you speak** with the added support of a simple visual. Advanced students need to hear you talk for 15 or 20 minutes when you first meet them to *get an ear* for how you sound. Intermediate students may need an hour or two, and beginners maybe a day or two. You could talk about cats for all I care, but the **History of English** is the best topic for all the reasons mentioned above. Using the timeline and the story of English as your introduction makes their learning space a safe, exciting place. It also establishes you as an expert and provides **context** for everything they have learned and everything they will learn.

Very soon, you'll be taking them to a galaxy far, far away. They need to believe in you and trust you. Share with them the **History of English** and they will.

Now that you have generated a good relationship with your students, my second strong suggestion is to ask them why they want to speak English? Their answers will shock you. Anything from I *want to go to school, get a job, some cute guy, speak at an international conference...* to the heart breaking *I want to talk to my grandchildren, who are growing up in America and they only speak English.* Now, can you imagine starting an English class without finding out why the students are learning English? Visit any English class in the world in my experience, this is not a common practice. The learners' needs provide the context for the course you are about to customize for them.

Now for the Meat and Potatoes.

Pronunciation

Sounds are the most basic units of oral communication, the building blocks.

The sound systems for the world's main languages have only two types of sounds: Consonant sounds where the air-flow out of the mouth is **stopped** or **restricted** (go ahead try a few /b/, /g/, /m/, /Sh/... see?), and Vowel sounds where the air flow is **unrestricted** (/Ayyyy/, /Eyyyy/, /Iyyyy/, /Owwww/...) See? All these years you have spoken/used/studied English and had no idea what made a consonant a consonant. I didn't know either until I was 40 and already a teacher. (My guru, Kathryn Brillinger, taught me.)

There are **24 consonant sounds** and **16 vowel sounds** in General American (GA) English. Don't be disheartened if you are British or Australian or South African... the patterns of English are the same in every version of English, which is why native English speakers from everywhere can understand one another (with a little exposure) even though there are a few variations in the sounds, words and expressions. These aren't problems.

A Functional Phonetic Alphabet (EPA)
First Tool in Your Traveling Teacher Toolbox

If you have been paying attention, and I think you have, you now know the ABC alphabet works for reading and writing but not speaking. We need an alphabet for speaking so we can *see* **what English sounds like.** If you are thinking, *What about IPA (International Phonetic Alphabet)?* I'm going to hunt you down and slap you. Here is my comment about IPA.

Do you know what this is?

It's a phone. It was invented in the 1800s, about the same time as IPA. The biggest difference between the telephone depicted here and IPA is that the ancient phone was at one time useful for English speakers. IPA never was. IPA was created for learning many languages. It's a cool idea, but unfortunately our only goal is English, and English is one language it doesn't work for. Rooted in French and Spanish, IPA's familiar letters **do not** represent **English** sounds (long e is /iy/ or /iː/, y is /j/, j is /dz/, th is /ɵ/ or /ð/ and so on...), ineffectively replacing one nonsense set of symbols with another. Ridiculous! As a translation step away from the target language, IPA was never useful for learning English. Not much tips a learner off that a teacher has no idea what they are doing than if they trot out IPA, unless it's uttering *Sound it out.* IPA is off the table as it is not a functional phonetic alphabet for English. It never was.

Most students are unfamiliar with any phonetic alphabet — bonus. Their first exposure will be with a useful one. However, if your students are Chinese, they already know IPA and are quite attached to it even though it hasn't done them a particle of good. Be respectful of all learners. Included in your toolbox is a phonetic alphabet chart with both EPA and IPA. Present the alphabets together if you like, and then let the student choose EPA in their own time. Since conversation is words following one after the other and IPA doesn't accommodate connected speech, Chinese speakers usually choose EPA the moment they have to speak.

CRACKING
THE CODE
BOOK ONE

2 EPA: The English Phonetic Alphabet

The best phonetic alphabet for English is the simplest, was created specifically for English, and uses only standard keyboard symbols. The English Phonetic Alphabet (EPA) also provides for consecutive words. Pretty much all conversation is words strung together, so it is super handy to finally have a phonetic system that visually represents exactly how native speakers talk to one another. No other phonetic alphabet does this.

So you have to learn a new alphabet. Don't worry, it won't take you long because it's logical and uses ABCs almost exclusively.

Written English = ABC, Spoken English = EPA.
Separate languages, two alphabets.

Sound Notation: The slash brackets mean /makes the sound/

This is a dog.

Woof

It makes the sound /woof/.

This is a **b**. It makes the sound /b/. Got it?

Consonant Sounds

You know there are 24 consonant sounds in GA English. 18 of them are represented exactly as one expects them to be. Let's harvest these from ABCs:

_, b, _, d, _, f, g, h, _, j, k, l, m, n, _, p, _, r, s, t, _, v, w, _, y, z

b	/b/	boy	**d**	/d/	dog	**f**	/f/	five
g	/g/	goat	**h**	/h/	house	**j**	/j/	July
k	/k/	king	**l**	/l/	lemon	**m**	/m/	money
n	/n/	number	**p**	/p/	people	**r**	/r/	red
s	/s/	summer	**t**	/t/	time	**v**	/v/	vest
w	/w/	woman	**y**	/y/	yellow	**z**	/z/	zebra

If you are doing the math, that leaves only 6 consonant sounds that you need to learn the symbols for. These common sounds are written down simply and logically — you've got this.

ch is /ch/ as in chair

sh is /sh/ as in shoe

th has two sounds - /TH/ as in thin and /Th/ as in then

ng is /Ng/ a common enough sound in words like finger and sing (and hidden in nk words like pink /piNgk/ and think /THiNgk/). No words begin with /Ng/ in English.

Zh is /zh/ as in genre. (Genre means category). English got it from French and there is no letter for /zh/. I had to pick genre as its representative word because genre is the only English word that begins with /zh/ but /zh/ is frequently found in the middle and end of words like pleasure, usual, garage and azure.

The consonant (stopped) sounds of English: 18 familiar - /b/, /d/, /f/, /g/, /h/, /j/, /k/, /l/, /m/, /n/, /p/, /r/, /s/, /t/, /v/, /w/, /y/, /z/ and 6 new - /ch/, /sh/, /TH/, /Th/, /Ng/, /zh/

That's it, you are done learning the phonetic symbols for English consonant sounds. Good job!

Please Note:

- There is no **c, q** or **x** in the phonetic alphabet because the sounds they make are all covered by other symbols. For example, c in city is /s/, in country is /k/, in cello is /ch/, in ocean is /sh/, in muscle it's silent; q is always /kw/; and x is either /ks/ as in expect, /gz/ as in exam and occasionally /z/ as in Xena, the warrior princess.

- **Capital letters** indicate two symbols represent one sound. It's important.

- When a **letter is silent,** the symbol is Ø.

Sample Consonant Sounds Exercise

On a separate piece of paper, write the EPA symbol / / for each of the underlined letters below: Example <u>ph</u>one /f/

Basic:

1	<u>n</u>ine	/ /		6	fa<u>c</u>e	/ /
2	<u>c</u>up	/ /		7	na<u>t</u>ion	/ /
3	<u>h</u>ome	/ /		8	no<u>s</u>e	/ /
4	<u>th</u>ink	/ /		9	orange	/ /
5	ne<u>ck</u>	/ /		10	s<u>ch</u>ool	/ /

Advanced:

1	so<u>c</u>ial	/ /		6	lis<u>t</u>en	/ /
2	A<u>s</u>ia	/ /		7	lang<u>u</u>age	/ /
3	pre<u>tt</u>y	/ /		8	sol<u>d</u>ier	/ /
4	ask<u>ed</u>	/ /		9	i<u>s</u>land	/ /
5	e<u>x</u>plain	/ /		10	on<u>i</u>on	/ /

FYI: There are more consonant sound exercises in ***English is Stupid, Students are Not*** and the ***English Phonetic Alphabet Workbook***, both available from Amazon.

Answer Key: Consonant Sounds

Basic: 1 /n/, 2 /k/, 3 /h/, 4 /TH/, 5 /k/, 6 /s/, 7 /sh/, 8 /z/, 9 /j/, 10 /k/

Advanced: 1 /sh/, 2 /zh/, 3 /d/, 4 /t/, 5 /ks/, 6 /Ø/, 7 /w/, 8 /j/, 9 /Ø/, 10 /y/

Vowel Sounds

There are props for this part. Vowel sounds stretch. Find a rubber/elastic band, hook it between your thumbs and pull your hands apart as you say the vowel sound /Ay/ as in gray. Stretch it out /Aaaayyyy/. Be prepared to demonstrate this to your students and provide them with their own rubber bands. Unrestricted sounds are **vowel sounds,** and there are 16 of them in GA English. The second tool in your toolbox is a class set of large, floppy elastic bands.

I've never had a student who didn't feel a little bit sick at this moment. They understood that there were 5 vowels in English a, e, i, o, u. Now we're telling them there are 16? Yup, there are 16 **vowel sounds**. And there is virtually no connection between the letters a, e, i, o, u and the 16 sounds. Any vowel or combination of vowels can represent any vowel sound at any time. I'll show you what I mean, and you will feel a bit sick too if you don't already.

Take **long a** and **short i** for example. There are more than a few ways to spell the **long a** sound /Ay/ as in gray, name, train, great, eight, they... It's the same for the **short i** sound /i/ as in pink, sit, busy, pretty, women, build, myth...

English spelling doesn't make sense, and vowels are worse than consonants. Don't lose heart; the solution is surprisingly simple.

To add insult to injury, all the rules you were taught in school about vowels are untrue. Shoot. I had intended not to trash traditional education anymore, but apparently I can't help myself. Other precepts you are familiar with are *i before e except after c* and *when two vowels go a walking, the first one does the talking* more absolute bunk! None of this stuff is true.

I BEFORE E EXCEPT AFTER C DISPROVED BY SCIENCE

It's not only confusing as heck for learners who are confronted daily with words like science, weird, eight, foreign, neighbor, beige, weight, sleigh, said, build, heart, guess, piece, field, enough... It's not only the words that confuse learners, it's their teacher's total disregard for the information staring them in the face. When a rule has thousands of exceptions, it isn't a rule! A rule is a rule when there are no exceptions. Another name for a rule with no exceptions is a pattern. **Patterns are the goal.**

EPA Color Vowels

The System that Makes Impossible English Pronunciation Possible

Oh, happy day! Coincidently, the 16 vowel sounds in English are central to the names of 16 ordinary colors. Colors provide the bridge to pronunciation that letters don't. *Color words* are a very simple, very effective way to elicit accurate pronunciation every time.

Even better, the names of colors are one of the first things a student learns in a new language. I took German in high school for three years because there was a cute boy in the class. We broke up 35 years ago and I haven't spoken German since, but I still remember that *Schwarz* is black, *Rot* is red, *Weiss* is white.... Introducing the patterns of speaking with the very first topic students learn gives every learner access to perfect pronunciation from day one. No other English speaking method does this.

The Thompson Vowel Chart for Vowel Sounds

The Most Valuable Paper ESL Students Will Ever Receive

The Thompson Vowel Chart holds the key to five of the six patterns of conversation: sounds, word stress, sentence stress, linking (connected speech), even expressions. But I'm getting ahead of myself. It suffices to say, learners should not leave home without this piece of paper. With this chart, a rubber band, a sharp stick and a flat stretch of dirt you will soon be able to teach people to speak English.

Up at the top, the word **Gray** holds the vowel sound **long a** /Ay/. Say it out loud. Can you hear the /Ay/ sound in Gray? Any word with the main vowel sound /Ay/ is considered a **Gray** word. Can you hear the /Ay/ sound in: rain, name, great, eight, nation, trade, weight, creation, face, date, maid? Did you say them out loud? Do it over.

Regardless of spelling, these words are all **Gray** words because their main vowel sound is /Ay/.

Long vowels are **long** because they contain **two sounds.**

THOMPSON VOWEL CHART

Color Word	Color	EPA	Double Example
gray		/Ay/	rainy day
black		/a/	black cat
green		/Ey/	green tree
red		/e/	red head
white		/Iy/	white knight
pink		/i/	pink ring
gold		/Ow/	old goat
olive		/o/	hot coffee
blue		/Uw/	blue shoe
mustard		/u/	honey mustard
wood		/^/	good wood
turquoise		/Oy/	noisy toy
brown		/Aw/	brown cow
purple		/Er/	purple girl
charcoal		/Ar/	dark charcoal
orange		/Or/	orange door

TLC THOMPSON LANGUAGE CENTER   Changing the way the world learns English.

Next, **short a** /a/ is the vowel sound in the word **black.** Any word with the main vowel sound /a/ is a **Black** word. Say them out loud. Can you hear the /a/ sound in c<u>a</u>t, h<u>a</u>lf, st<u>a</u>ff, l<u>au</u>gh, pl<u>ai</u>d, f<u>a</u>st, re<u>a</u>ct, s<u>a</u>d? These are all **black** words because their main vowel sound is /a/.

Recap:

Rain, made, maid, rein and reign are **Gray.** Had, cat, half, staff and laugh are **Black** because of their *sound,* not their spelling. **The colour vowel connection** is a system for accessing pronunciation in spite of crazy spelling. Most of you can already see how the system works, but we'll do a few more to seal the deal.

Long e /Ey/ is the vowel sound in **green.** Can you hear /Ey/ in tr<u>ee</u>, m<u>e</u>, s<u>ea</u>t, p<u>eo</u>ple, p<u>ie</u>ce, th<u>e</u>se, rec<u>ei</u>pt, sk<u>i</u>? These are all **Green** words because the main vowel sound is /Ey/.

Short e /e/ is the vowel sound in **red.** Can you hear /e/ in b<u>e</u>d, h<u>ea</u>d, s<u>ai</u>d, fr<u>ie</u>nd, g<u>ue</u>st? These are all **Red** words because the main vowel sound is /e/.

As for the rest of the vowel sounds...

Long i /ly/ is in **white:** five, my, pie, height, buy, bye, by, I, eye, aye, isle, I'll, aisle   **White** words

Short i /i/ is in **pink:** is, it, in, sister, build, pretty, busy, women, English, history   **Pink** words

Long o /ow/ is in **gold:** nose, toast, toe, those, know, beau, sew, though, ghost   **Gold** words

Short o /o/ is in **olive** (dirty green): hot, coffee, father, caught, broad, cough, awe, law   **Olive** words

Long u /uw/ is in **blue:** to, two, too, new, you, through, beautiful, glue, shoe, school, fuel   **Blue** words

Short u /u/ is in **mustard** (dirty yellow): bus, from, was, the, flood, does, because, mother   **Mustard** words

/^/ **Wood:** put, could, look, woman   **Wood**

/oy/ **Turquoise:** boy, noise, loyal, lawyer   **Turquoise**

/aw/ **Brown:** now, town, vowel, sound   **Brown**

R Vowels:

/Er/ **Purple:** her, first, nurse, word, were, heard, thirty   **Purple**

/Ar/ **Charcoal** (dark gray): car, park, heart, are, R, market   **Charcoal**

/or/ **Orange:** door, four, more, war, coarse   **Orange**

This is the system. **Color names** classify all the English **vowel sounds** and provide a link to **pronunciation** in spite of crazy spelling. Students learn the color of each word when they learn vocabulary. It's a small price to pay for the speaking confidence and freedom this system provides.

FYI: *How Do You Say?* is a dictionary for **Expressions, Pronunciation** and **Spelling**. It's based on the **Thompson Vowel Chart** and the first English dictionary that categorizes vocabulary by sound, not spelling. It's really cool. Available on Amazon.

The 16 Vowel Sounds of English in a Nutshell

- **The first 10 vowel sounds: Long** and **short a** are **Gray** /ᴀy/ and **Black** /a/; **long** and **short e** are **Green** /ᴇy/ and **Red** /e/; **long** and **short i** are **White** /ɪy/ and **Pink** /i/; **long** and **short o** are **Gold** /ow/ and **Olive** /o/; **long** and **short u** are **Blue** /ᴜw/ and **Mustard** /u/ just to help you keep track.

Did you notice long vowels have two symbols in them? That's what makes them long.

Did you notice it is either a **w** or a **y** that makes long vowels long? Remember this because these are really going to shine in connected speech (talking) in Book Two on *Conversation.*

- The next 3 vowel sounds are **Wood** /^/, **Turquoise** /oy/ and **Brown** /ᴀw/. I call them orphans because they don't belong to any other group.

- R is a stiff sound that profoundly affects the vowel sound next to it. In three cases, R causes new sounds known as R *Vowels*: **Purple** /ᴇr/, **Charcoal** (dark gray) /ᴀr/ and **Orange** /or/.

- Words that end in vowel sounds, end in long vowel sounds not short ones.

Sample Vowel Sounds Exercise

On a separate piece of paper, write the EPA symbol / / for each of the underlined letters below: Example: n<u>a</u>me /ᴀy/

Basic

1	n<u>o</u>	/ /		6	t<u>ow</u>n	/ /
2	r<u>oa</u>d	/ /		7	f<u>a</u>ther	/ /
3	h<u>a</u>t	/ /		8	n<u>oi</u>se	/ /
4	l<u>au</u>gh	/ /		9	f<u>i</u>rst	/ /
5	d<u>oor</u>	/ /		10	gr<u>ea</u>t	/ /

Advanced

1	s<u>ai</u>d	/ /		6	w<u>o</u>men	/ /
2	b<u>ui</u>ld	/ /		7	p<u>ea</u>ce	/ /
3	p<u>ie</u>	/ /		8	j<u>ui</u>ce	/ /
4	c<u>ou</u>ld	/ /		9	h<u>ea</u>rt	/ /
5	m<u>o</u>ther	/ /		10	<u>o</u>f	/ /

Answer Key: Vowel Sounds

Basic: 1 /ow/ gold, 2 /ow/ gold, 3 /a/ black, 4 /a/ black, 5 /or/ orange, 6 /Aw/ brown, 7 /o/ olive, 8 /oy/ turquoise, 9 /Er/ purple, 10 /Ay/ gray

Advanced: 1 /e/ red, 2 /i/ pink, 3 /Iy/ white, 4 /^/ wood, 5 /u/ mustard, 6 /i/ pink, 7 /Ey/ green, 8 /Uw/ blue, 9 /Ar/ charcoal, 10 /u/ mustard

Blank Vowel Chart Student Exercise

The Thompson Vowel Chart is the most important piece of paper learners will ever receive, but what if you don't have access to a photocopier? Or the photo copier you do have access to prints only black and white? No problem. Have them make their own in an assembly line. The Blank Thompson Vowel Chart template is included in your tool kit.

THOMPSON VOWEL CHART

color word	color	EPA	double example
gray		/Ay/	rainy day
black		/a/	black cat
green		/Ey/	green tree
red		/e/	red head
white		/Iy/	white knight
pink		/I/	pink ring
gold		/ow/	old goat
olive		/o/	hot coffee
blue		/Uw/	blue shoe
mustard		/u/	honey mustard
wood		/^/	good wood
turquoise		/oy/	noisy toy
brown		/Aw/	brown cow
purple		/Er/	purple girl
charcoal		/Ar/	dark charcoal
orange		/or/	orange door

COLORED PENCILS

FYI: Olive, Mustard and Turquoise pencils are the hardest to find. Staples brand has them.

33

Actually, black and white photocopies of the blank Thompson Vowel Chart are really, really handy. If you are tutoring one or two students, have them color their own. If you have a class, then give the first student the stack of blank copies and a gray colored pencil. The first student will color the gray rectangle on each page and, Henry Ford style, as they finish each page, hand it to the next student who will color in the black rectangle; the next student, green; the next, red... until it's done.

It's a fantastic exercise because the students get to contribute and, even better, spend fifteen minutes or so just being with the paper. It's visual, it's kinetic, it's not too difficult, it's important... You know what? Even if you have access to a color photocopier, don't print the EPA Color Vowel chart out in color to hand out to students. They will miss out on a lot by not being part of the process of creating the chart. (When I'm tutoring business executives, I hand them a photocopy of the chart. Everyone else, even foreign-trained professionals, they color their own charts.)

All Vowel Sounds are Not Equally Difficult

If you are feeling overwhelmed with the 16 vowel sounds, don't be. All vowel sounds are not equally difficult. Languages usually have the long vowels but are missing the short ones.

The Four Most Difficult Vowels

Short o – Olive, **short u** – Mustard, **short i** – Pink and the R vowel Purple are the most difficult sounds for non-native speakers from almost every language background. **Short a** – **Black** is the next hardest, and maybe **short e** – Red, but these are the worst of it.

Hot Tip: I use *Hop on Pop* by Dr. Seuss to reinforce vowel sounds in authentic material. Each page focuses on a different vowel sound. **Put a copy in your tool box.**

If any instructor or student balks at using a children's book because they fear it may belittle the learner or the lesson, I'm going to tell you a little story. A brilliant 45-year-old man of Chinese descent was both a lawyer and an engineer. He was employed as an engineer in Canada, but his speaking was so difficult to understand, I was hired to make him intelligible. I was given three months, one hour a week, to do it or his contract would be terminated.

Chinese speakers often have difficulty with some specific sounds, for example /l/ and /r/, and often consonant sounds at the ends of words are not pronounced at all. If I were asked, *How many for dinner?*, I might respond, *Six for dinner*. But my engineer/lawyer friend would respond, *Si fo dinna*. His accent was fossilized; he had spoken this way for a long, long time.

I gave him a copy of **Hop on Pop** (Ho o Po) for his very own after I'd underlined the final consonants and dog-eared the pages with his specific sound challenges. He looked at the book and said, *This book is too juvenile for me,* indicating the high level of his English.

I responded, *Yes, it is juvenile. When you can read it, I'll give you another book.*

It took him two weeks to be able to read **Hop on Pop** aloud perfectly, after which he said, *This author is fantastic! Did he write anything else?* He kept his job.

Bear in mind, your students have never studied anything useful about speaking. They are all beginners. Just because a student is advanced, you can't pull out law articles or metallurgy handbooks to start teaching them to speak. Even advanced students went off the tracks on day one, and the very beginning is where all learners have to start. The only difference between the program for advanced students and the program for beginner students is the amount of time they spend in each phase. Advanced students can grasp this material as quickly as a native speaker putting it into practice takes a little longer.

The Thompson Vowel Chart Value Proposition

What the Thompson Vowel chart supplies is a blueprint, and it's portable. Learners can take it with them wherever they go, and they can capture the correct pronunciation of words they encounter without a teacher. They are mobile and empowered. Capability and independence — isn't this what education is really about?

Sneak Preview: In the next part, I'll show you an easy way to determine which sounds consonants and vowels are different between English and any learner's first language. This is another way of saying that you can customize a list of English sounds your learner needs to concentrate on.

Footnote: Color Options

- /i/ Some accents don't pronounce a **short i** in **pink,** and it sounds like a green word /pEyngk/. If there is no /i/ in pink the way you pronounce it, then choose another color word like indigo or silver to house /i/ in your lessons.

- /oy/ You may choose oyster (grayish brownish) as a better color word for /oy/ as /oy/ is not the main vowel sound in the word Turquoise, it just makes a prettier chart! Using turquoise for /oy/ doesn't confuse students, so I stick with it. You do what you like.

- RP is British English (Received Pronunciation). RP has more than 16 vowel sounds. For example, Dawn and Don sound the same in GA but not in RP. Modify your chart to include /Au/ Auburn (redbrown) if it reflects your accent more accurately. Something different happens with the R vowels in RP, too. I add Clear /Eyr/ and Pear /Ayr/ for British English (RP), but you get the idea. The name of a color has to house the vowel sound to create a key that helps learners remember how to pronounce words regardless of spelling.

Recap

- Understand and unequivocally accept that English writing and English speaking are different languages.

- EPA is a set of keyboard symbols that logically represents English sounds so learners can **see** what English **sounds** like.

Transcriptions

On a separate piece of paper, transcribe the following words from spoken English to written English. Check your answers at the end of the chapter.

Basic

1	/dʌyt/		6	/towz/
2	/piŋgk/		7	/nɛy/
3	/flyv/		8	/skʊwl/
4	/ʌyt/		9	/iz/
5	/wun/		10	/shugɛr/

Advanced

1	/f^t/		6	/skwʌyer/
2	/bɛrd/		7	/unyun/
3	/kwɛyn/		8	/bowt/
4	/uv/		9	/sidɛy/
5	/ges/		10	/wuns/

Answer Key: Transcriptions

Basic: 1 date, **2** pink, **3** five, **4** eight/ate, **5** one/won, **6** toes/tows, **7** knee, **8** school, **9** is, **10** sugar

Advanced: 1 foot, **2** bird, **3** queen, **4** of, **5** guess, **6** square, **7** onion, **8** boat, **9** city, **10** once

3 Tools to Compare English Sounds to the Sounds of Any Other Language

Worth the Price of Admission

Venn Diagrams are a super handy tool for comparing languages.

Do you know anything about Venn Diagrams? They compare sets and show where those sets intersect. Because you are learning how to compare languages, Venns are about to become your new best friend. We'll start with a simple practice Venn to be sure we are all on the same page.

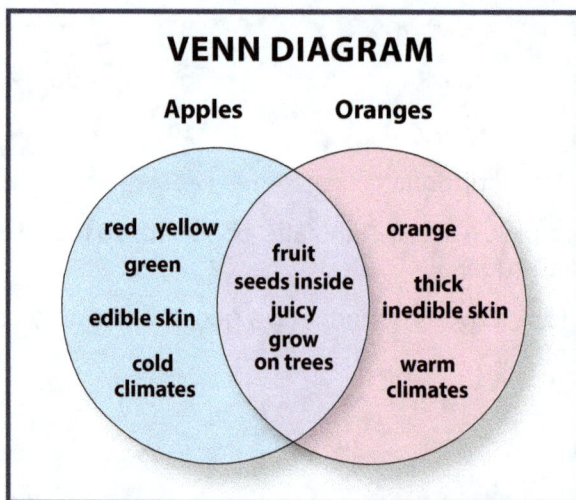

VENN DIAGRAM

Apples   Oranges

red   yellow
green
edible skin
cold
climates

fruit
seeds inside
juicy
grow
on trees

orange
thick
inedible skin

warm
climates

Some things that are different about apples and oranges are colors, skin qualities, and where they grow, evidenced by the blue space on the left and the pink space on the right no contact. Some things that are the same about apples and oranges are that they are both juicy fruits with seeds inside that grow on trees. This information is in the purple section in the middle shared qualities. Got it? If you don't, do some research on the internet because this is key.

Just for fun, here is a comparison of the units of written and spoken English. The complete circle on the left contains the 26 letters of the alphabet were you to add them up. The complete circle on the right contains the 40 sounds in GA English. Consonants above the center line and vowels below.

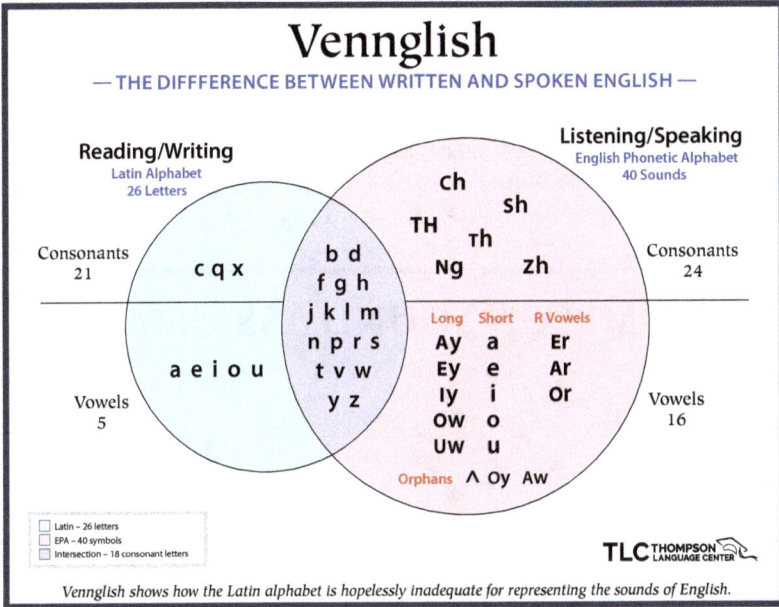

Vennglish
— THE DIFFFERENCE BETWEEN WRITTEN AND SPOKEN ENGLISH —

Reading/Writing
Latin Alphabet
26 Letters

Listening/Speaking
English Phonetic Alphabet
40 Sounds

Consonants
21

Consonants
24

c q x

b d
f g h
j k l m
n p r s
t v w
y z

ch
sh
TH
Th
Ng   zh

a e i o u

Long	Short	R Vowels
Ay	a	Er
Ey	e	Ar
Iy	i	Or
Ow	o	
Uw	u	

Vowels
5

Vowels
16

Orphans Λ Oy Aw

☐ Latin – 26 letters
☐ EPA – 40 symbols
☐ Intersection – 18 consonant letters

TLC THOMPSON LANGUAGE CENTER

Vennglish shows how the Latin alphabet is hopelessly inadequate for representing the sounds of English.

The 18 symbols in the purple section in the middle are the ones we talked about, the 18 consonants that make the sound one expects them to make. These 18 symbols are the place where the written English alphabet (EPA) and the spoken English (ABC) alphabet intersect.

Notice:

- c, q and x in the upper left section are used in writing, not speaking

- a, e, i, o, u in the lower left section are meaningless in speaking, their connection to sounds is too loose to be of any service

- in the pink upper right section are the 6 new symbols for the unrepresented consonants

- in the pink lower right are the phonetic symbols for the 16 vowel sounds in English 10 of the long and shorts, 3 orphans and 3 R vowels.

FYI: 2' X 3' classroom poster PDFs are available of the charts in this book from thompsonlanguagecenter.com

The Rubber Hits the Road

Putting to Use What You Have Learned So Far

The Assessment

How can EPA and Venn Diagrams be used to determine the sound differences between English and the language your student/students are speaking? Easy! I made this assessment tool for you. The 40 sounds of GA English that we just studied **start out** in the purple section in the middle of the Venn. The assessment is a joint activity between you (the English expert) and your student, the expert in some other language.

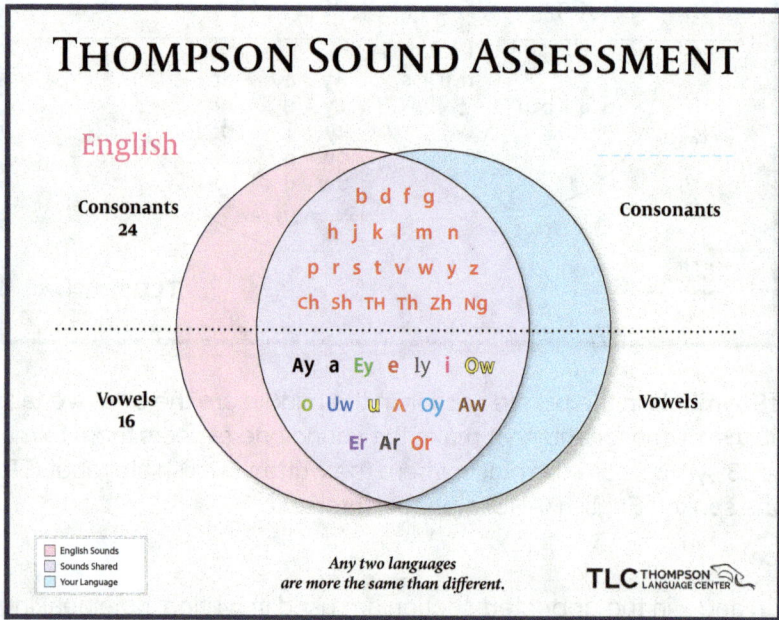

THOMPSON SOUND ASSESSMENT

English

Consonants 24

Consonants

b d f g
h j k l m n
p r s t v w y z
ch sh TH Th Zh Ng

Ay a Ey e ly i Ow
o Uw U ʌ Oy Aw
Er Ar Or

Vowels 16

Vowels

English Sounds
Sounds Shared
Your Language

*Any two languages
are more the same than different.*

TLC THOMPSON LANGUAGE CENTER

Together you start at the top with /b/. Say the sound out loud and have your student declare either "Yes, /b/ is a sound in my language," in which case **leave it where it is**

or

"No, that sound is not in my language," in which case you **take the sound out of the purple section and move it to the left into the pink section** of English Consonants.

Next, /d/ say the sound out loud and have your student declare either "Yes, /d/ is in my language," in which case **leave it where it is**

or

"No, that sound is not in my language," in which case you **take the sound out of the purple section and move it to the left into the pink section** of English Consonants.

Follow this process with every English sound in the purple section. The goal is to isolate all the sounds in English that are not in the learner's first language in the pink crescent on the left. You will end up with a diagram that looks something like this:

English/Spanish Venn

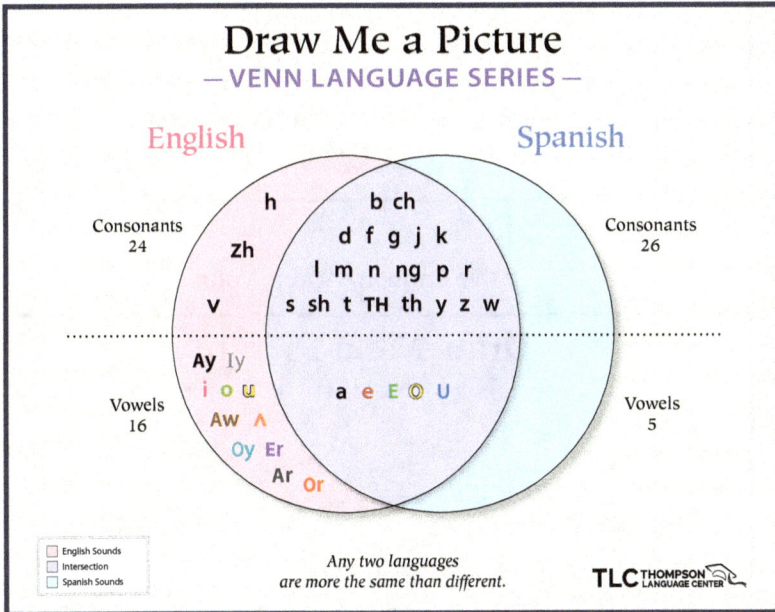

Draw Me a Picture
— VENN LANGUAGE SERIES —

English   Spanish

Consonants 24

Consonants 26

h   b ch
Zh   d f g j k
      l m n ng p r
v   s sh t TH th y z w

Vowels 16

Ay Iy
i o u
Aw ʌ   a e E O U
Oy Er
Ar Or

Vowels 5

English Sounds
Intersection
Spanish Sounds

Any two languages
are more the same than different.

TLC THOMPSON LANGUAGE CENTER

Or this **English/French Venn**

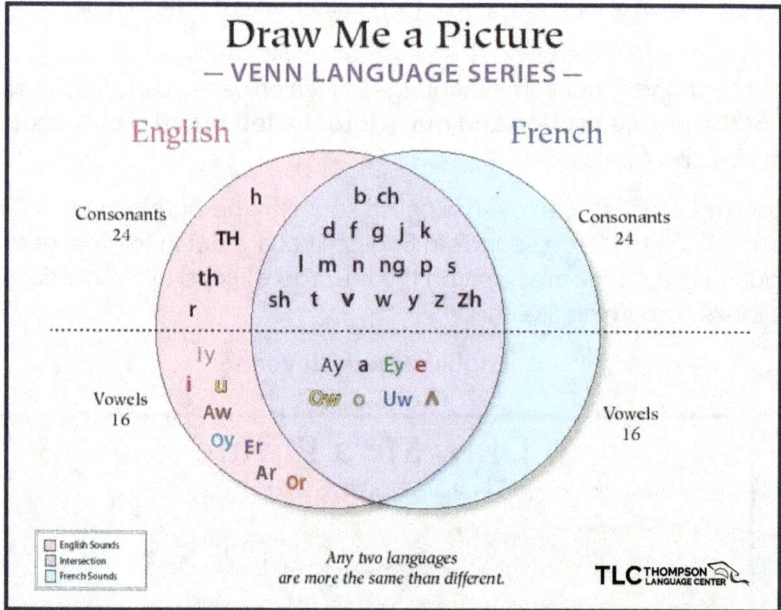

Draw Me a Picture
— VENN LANGUAGE SERIES —

English   French

Consonants
24

Consonants
24

h   b ch
TH   d f g j k
th   l m n ng p s
r   sh t v w y z Zh

Iy   Ay a Ey e
i u   Ow o Uw A
Aw
Oy Er
Ar Or

Vowels
16

Vowels
16

☐ English Sounds
☐ Intersection
☐ French Sounds

*Any two languages
are more the same than different.*

TLC THOMPSON LANGUAGE CENTER

Or this **English/Arabic Venn**

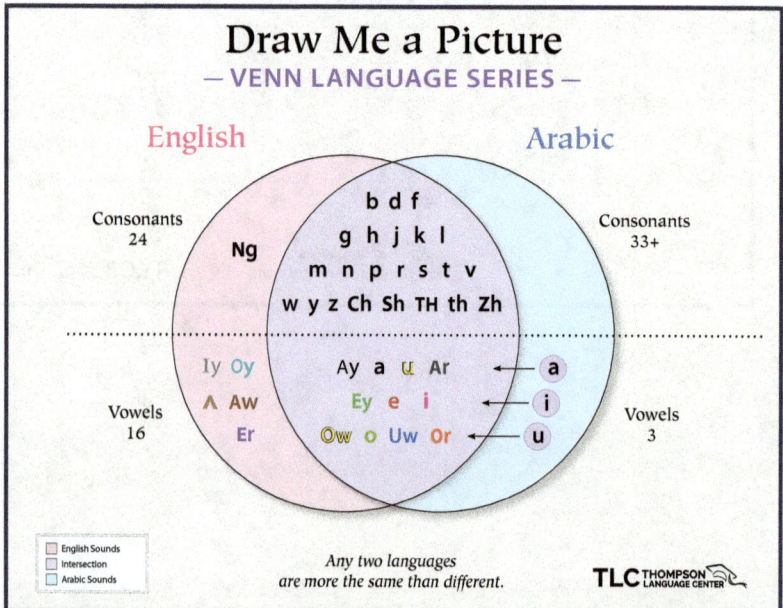

Draw Me a Picture
— VENN LANGUAGE SERIES —

English   Arabic

Consonants
24

Consonants
33+

Ng   b d f
     g h j k l
    m n p r s t v
   w y z Ch Sh TH th Zh

Iy Oy   Ay a u Ar ← a
ʌ Aw   Ey e i ← i
Er   Ow o Uw Or ← u

Vowels
16

Vowels
3

☐ English Sounds
☐ Intersection
☐ Arabic Sounds

*Any two languages
are more the same than different.*

TLC THOMPSON LANGUAGE CENTER

Or this **English/Mandarin Chinese Venn**

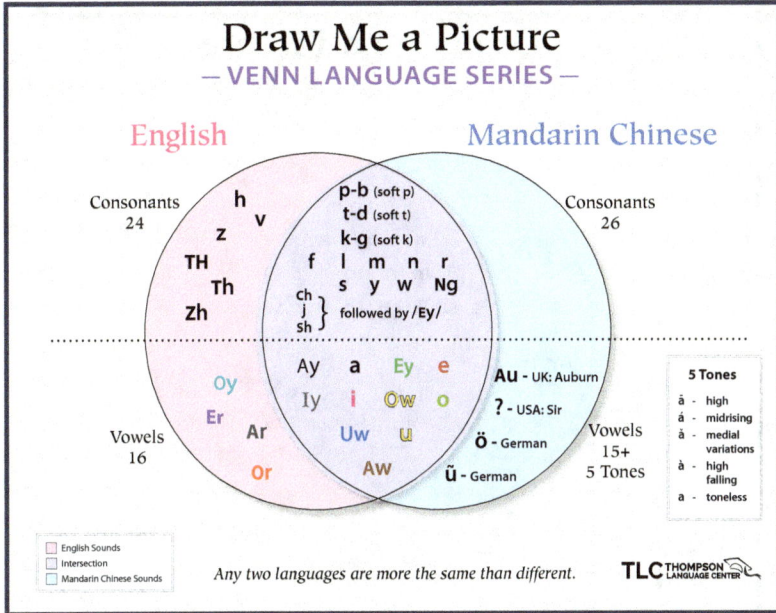

Draw Me a Picture
— VENN LANGUAGE SERIES —

English   Mandarin Chinese

Consonants 24   h   v   z   TH   Th   Zh

p-b (soft p)
t-d (soft t)
k-g (soft k)
f   l   m   n   r
ch } s   y   w   Ng
j } followed by /**Ey**/
sh }

Consonants 26

Oy   Er   Ar   Or

Ay   a   Ey   e
Iy   i   Ow   o
Uw   u
Aw

Au - UK: Auburn
? - USA: Sir
Ö - German
ü - German

Vowels 16

Vowels 15+ 5 Tones

5 Tones
ā - high
á - midrising
ǎ - medial variations
à - high falling
a - toneless

☐ English Sounds
☐ Intersection
☐ Mandarin Chinese Sounds

Any two languages are more the same than different.

TLC THOMPSON LANGUAGE CENTER

* Spanish, French, Arabic and Mandarin sound information taken from online IPA sites

What you are starting to notice is that most of the sounds remain in the purple center. Yeah! These are the sounds you don't have to teach. They are common to both English and the learner's first language. How encouraging for students to see all the work they don't have to do! The blue moon on the right is the space for the sounds in the first language that we don't need to worry about because we aren't learning that language; we only care about English in this course. If you want, you could fill in those spaces, but I'm not sure why, unless it helps you understand the big picture better.

English/Spanish Venn Full Comparison

One by one, go through the entire set of English sounds in the purple section. Sounds common to both languages stay where they are. Sounds that exist in English but not in the learner's first language go to the pink crescent on the left, creating the family of individual sounds the learner has to study. Sounds that exist in the first language but aren't found in the purple center go to the right. Once in a blue moon (I just wanted to say that), the learner can see the extra sounds in their own language, not in English, that they don't have to think about at all.

English/Spanish Venn

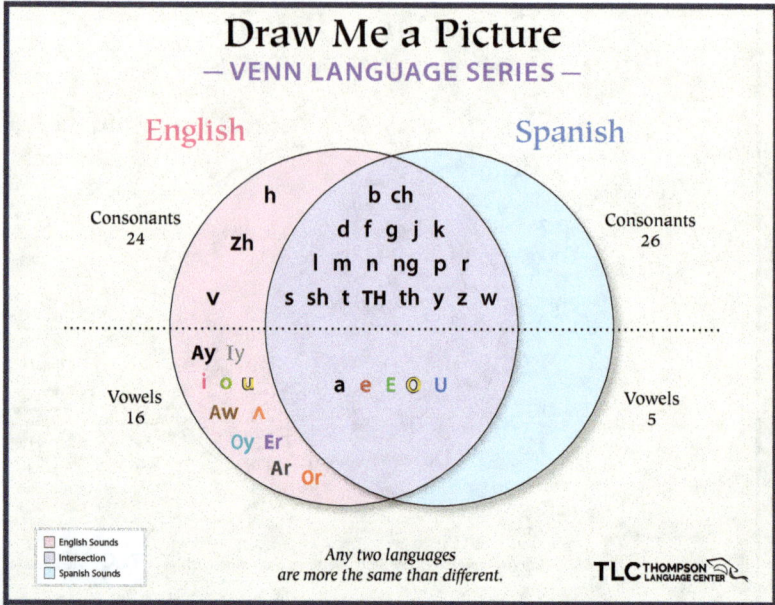

Draw Me a Picture
— VENN LANGUAGE SERIES —

English   Spanish

Consonants 24

Consonants 26

h   b ch
Zh   d f g j k
l m n ng p r
v   s sh t TH th y z w

Vowels 16

Ay Iy
i o u
Aw ʌ   a e E O U
Oy Er
Ar Or

Vowels 5

English Sounds
Intersection
Spanish Sounds

Any two languages
are more the same than different.

TLC THOMPSON LANGUAGE CENTER

In the English/Spanish Venn, you can see that Spanish has a few extra consonant sounds that are not used in English, and you can also see Spanish has no extra vowel sounds. As mentioned, the pink wedge on the left is the fascinating part. You can see in the top left that a Spanish student needs to work on a few extra consonant sounds, but by far the biggest area of focus for Spanish students is the bottom left wedge English vowel sounds.

I wouldn't try to teach Spanish speakers from the sample chart in this book because the information came from the IPA website and you already know what a dysfunctional resource that is. Do the work. It takes 15 minutes. Create the chart for your student, with your student. Because of their accent and yours... it will look slightly different from the chart I made.

Your Secret Agenda

The main reason for creating a sound chart one-to-one with your student has nothing to do academically with their learning. Truth be told, individual sounds are not really important in English conversation (more on this in Book Two). What you get out of the exercise is, first and foremost, credibility. Any learner is going to take a flyer on lessons from a native English speaker, save some money and hope beyond hope that the random traveler can make a difference for them. Imagine their shock and joy when in the first lesson with you makes more of a difference than any program they have suffered through so far?

When you take ten or fifteen minutes and show that you can customize an English program for their specific accent, their world shifts; you gain standing, a working knowledge of their personal strengths and weaknesses, and trust. These are the invaluable hidden bonuses of creating a Venn with your students.

To create a customized English Venn for any language, visit the IPA site for that language and do the comparison yourself. Did we finally find a use for IPA?! No, not really. You don't have to use the crazy symbols; you can check the keywords instead. Close though we almost found a use for it.

Conclusion

It's a new day in English education. This revolutionary way to teach English considers the sounds and language skills each learner has and captures what is the same between English and their first language. The previously insurmountable problem with English was the disparity between its written and spoken forms. They are unbridged by a logical alphabet. English learners had no way **to see** how English was pronounced. The problem found a simple solution in EPA, the English Phonetic Alphabet, a phonetic alphabet for speaking.

Traditional English Pronunciation classes are being phased out leaving the door wide open for Backpackers with special specific training to help people in simpler more effective ways. Today, we know what went wrong with English, how to manage it for our students, as well as how to harness the similarities between first language and English in order to facilitate English language learning. As the international *lingua franca* (common language), nearly two billion people worldwide use English in some form. Native English speakers everywhere are frequently entreated to teach their mother tongue with no formal training whatsoever. With the *Backpacker's Guide to Teaching English*, now they can.

CRACKING THE CODE
BOOK ONE

Traveling Teacher Toolbox

EPA English Phonetic Alphabet Chart*

EPA IPA Chart*

Thompson Vowel Chart*

Economy size package of giant (6" recommended) rubber bands

Blank Thompson Vowel Chart*

Box of colored pencils (eg. Staples)

16 selected paint chips from local hardware store to represent the vowel colors

Hop on Pop **by Dr. Seuss**

*Available as free downloads from thompsonlanguagecenter.com

Notes